STUART
TIMES

GW00647951

CHESTS

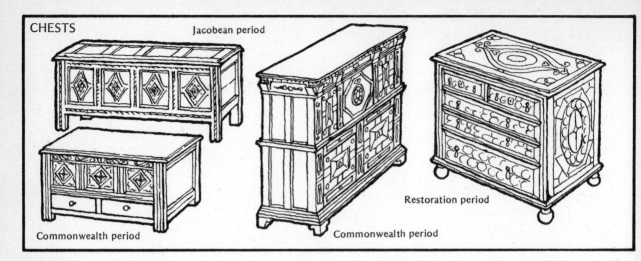

Jacobean period

Commonwealth period

Commonwealth period

Restoration period

DAYBEDS AND SETTEES

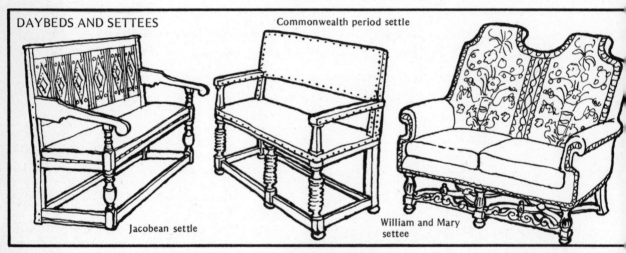

Commonwealth period settle

Jacobean settle

William and Mary settee

CHAIRS

Commonwealth period

Restoration period

William and Mary period

Jacobean period

William and Mary period

Queen Anne period

PRESSES AND CUPBOARDS

Restoration period

Jacobean period

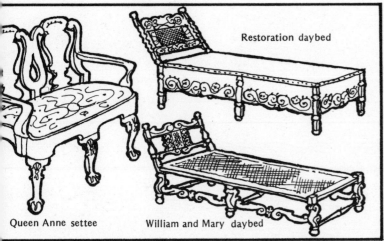

Restoration daybed

Queen Anne settee

William and Mary daybed

STOOLS

Jacobean period

early
Jacobean period

William and Mary period

TABLES

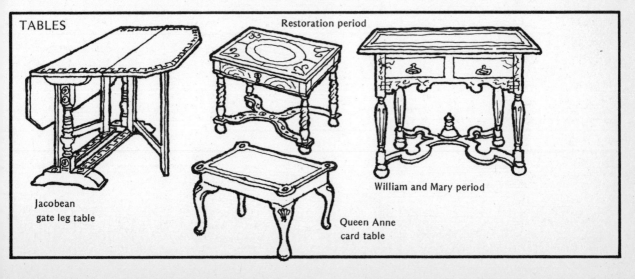

Restoration period

Jacobean
gate leg table

Queen Anne
card table

William and Mary period

Ham House staircase

room setting

Cavalier

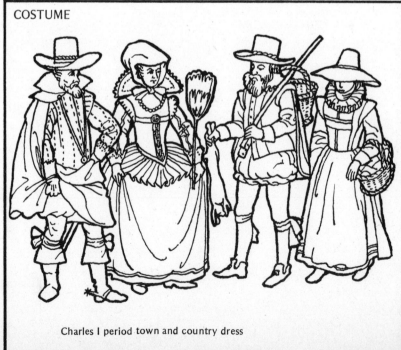

COSTUME

Charles I period town and country dress

METALWARE

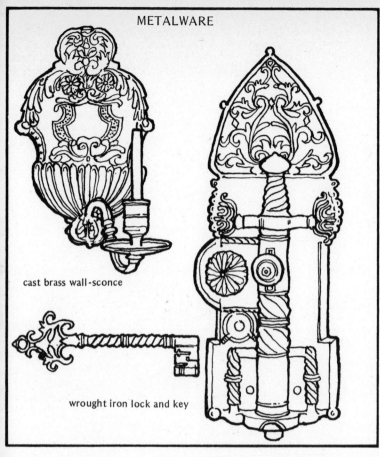

cast brass wall-sconce

wrought iron lock and key

BEDROOM

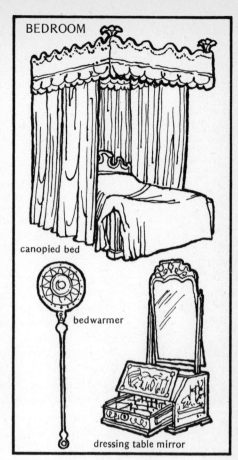

canopied bed

bedwarmer

dressing table mirror

Puritan dress

Late Stuart period

Roundhead

dying

collecting bodies

burying the dead

The Diseases and Casualties this Week.

Disease	Count	Disease	Count
Abortive	6	Kingsevil	10
Aged	54	Lethargy	1
Apoplexie	1	Murthered at Stepney	1
Bedridden	1	Palsie	2
Cancer	2	Plague	3880
Childbed	23	Plurisie	1
Chrisomes	15	Quinsie	6
Collick	1	Rickets	23
Consumtion	174	Rising of the Lights	19
Convulsion	88	Rupture	2
Dropsie	40	Sciatica	1
Drownd two, one at St Kath. Tower, and one at Lambeth	2	Scowring	13
		Scurvy	1
Feaver	353	Sore Legge	1
Fistula	1	Spotted Feaver and Purples	190
Flox and Small-pox	10	Starved at Nurse	1
Flux	2	Stilborn	8
Found dead in the Street at St Bartholomew the Less	1	Stone	2
		Stopping of the Stomach	16
Frighted	1	Strangury	1
Gangrene	1	Suddenly	1
Gowt	1	Surfeit	87
Grief	1	Teeth	113
Griping in the Guts	74	Thrush	3
Jaundies	3	Tissick	6
Imposthume	18	Ulcer	2
Infants	21	Vomiting	7
Killed by a fall downstairs at St Thomas Apostle	1	Winde	8
		Wormes	18

Bills of Mortality

corpse bearers

fleeing the city

CRAFTSMEN

tailor

saddler

soap maker

STREET VENDORS

ballad seller

sausage seller

chicken man

SERVICES

cresset bearer

town crier

porter

chimney sweep

rat catcher

making paper

binding books

COLONIAL SLAVERY

planting

carting and loading cane

refining sugar

HUNTING

shooting birds

netting birds

fishing

HUNTING SWORDS

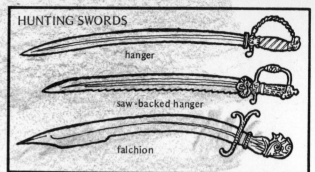

hanger

saw-backed hanger

falchion

players and musicians

pell-mell

Queen Anne playing cards

TOYS

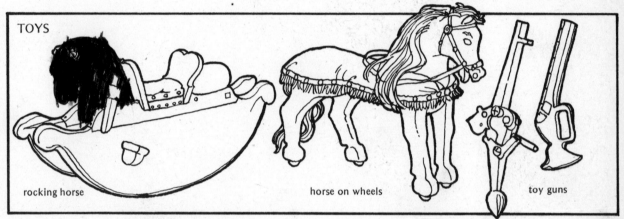

rocking horse

horse on wheels

toy guns

Vauxhall Pleasure Gardens

taking the waters at Bath

coffee house

frost fair on the Thames

horse racing

ON LAND

stage wagon

travelling coach

dray

sedan chair

highwayman attacking coach

postboy

early newspaper

The *Sovereign of the Seas*

coal barge

Thames ferry

royal barge

Bristol docks

fire hooks

squirt

leather buckets

THE MONARCHY

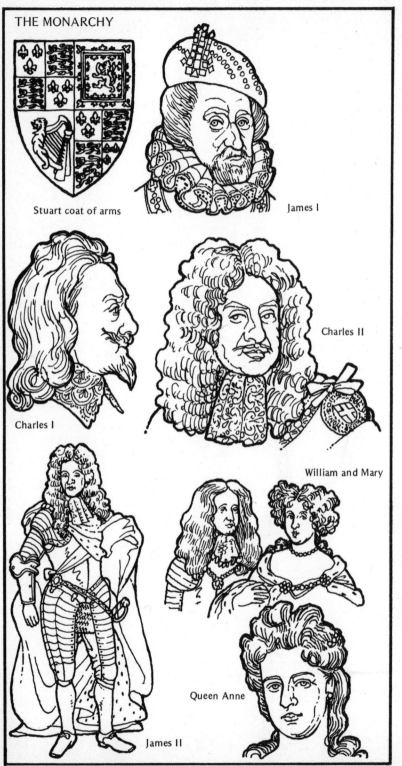

Stuart coat of arms

James I

Charles I

Charles II

William and Mary

Queen Anne

James II

Lord Mayor of London

Samuel Pepys Secretary of the Navy

CHARLES I

the trial

Charles I demands the five MPs

the execution

THE COMMONWEALTH

Commonwealth
coat of arms

Oliver Cromwell dissolves 'Rump' Parliament

John Churchill

Battle of Sedgemoor

Prince Rupert

Judge Jeffries giving judgement

GUNPOWDER PLOT

the conspirators: R. Winter   C. Wright   J. Wright   Percy   Fawkes   Catesby   T. Winter

Fawkes lays trail
— was there really a plot?

Fawkes arrested

THE AMERICAN COLONIES

American Indians

American Pilgrims

STUART TIMES Military Life

WEAPONS

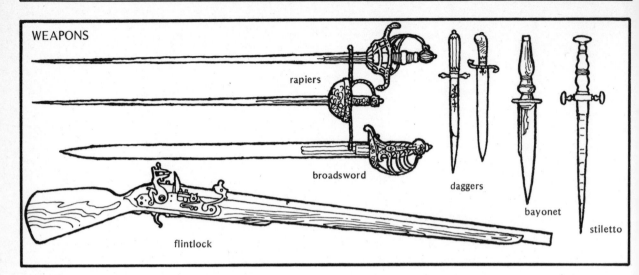

rapiers

broadsword

daggers

bayonet

stiletto

flintlock

ornamental drum

Dunbar medal

SHOOTING A MATCHLOCK

try match

pull out
scouring stick

SOLDIERS

musketeer

New Model trooper

pikeman

New Model officer

trooper

Campbell

Glencoe massacre

ram
bullet in   guard the pan   blow off
                                          loose powder   return match   fire

Coldstream Guard   cavalryman

SEAMEN

naval officer   wounded ordinary seaman

Dutch Wars

Cromwell's troops at Naseby

JAMES II AND IRELAND

James II lands in Ireland

Battle of the Boyne

Tallard surrenders to Marlborough at Blenheim

QUAKERS

meeting house

George Fox

Archbishop Laud

anti-Catholic hysteria

SCOTLAND

signing the Covenant

prayer book revolt

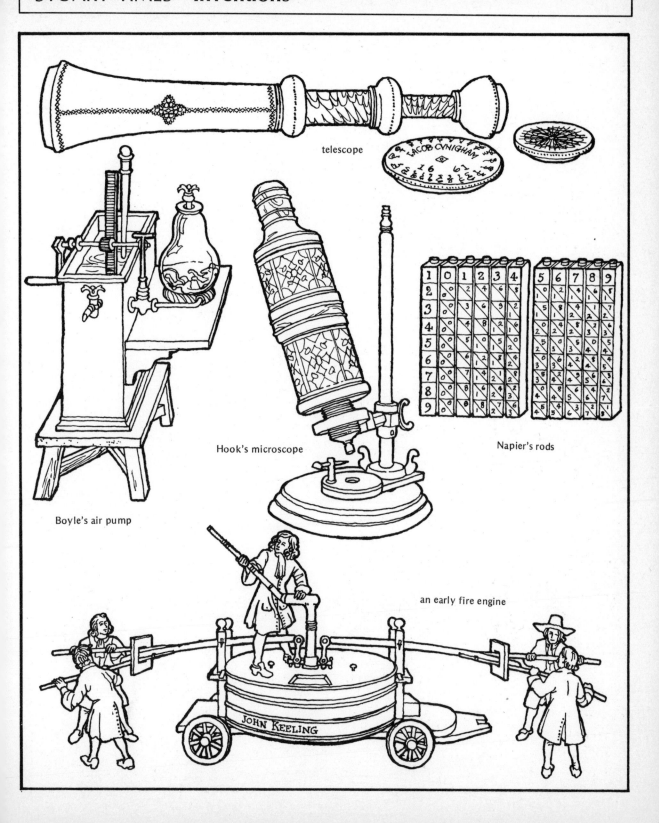

telescope

Boyle's air pump

Hook's microscope

Napier's rods

an early fire engine

JOHN KEELING

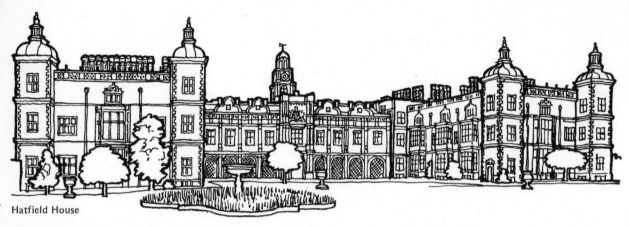

Hatfield House

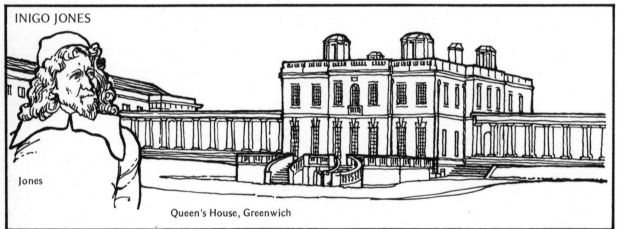

INIGO JONES

Jones

Queen's House, Greenwich

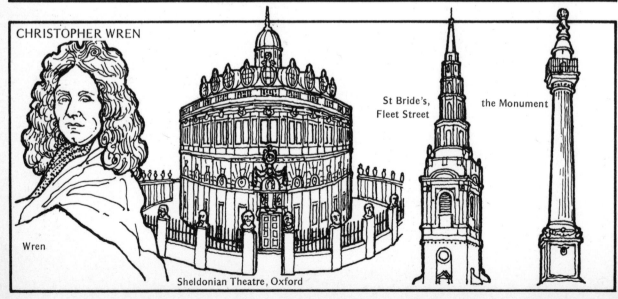

CHRISTOPHER WREN

Wren

Sheldonian Theatre, Oxford

St Bride's, Fleet Street

the Monument

firemark

Hawksmoor church, Spitalfields

draining the Fens

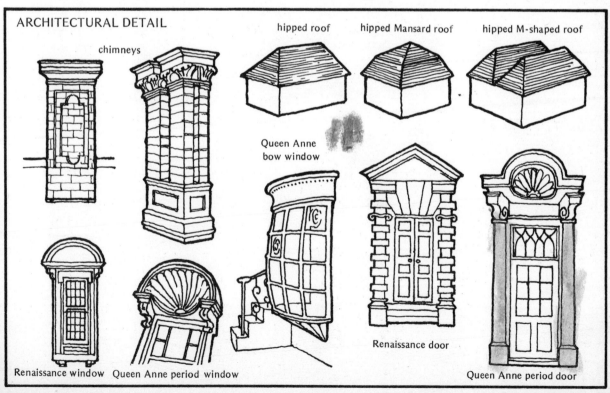

ARCHITECTURAL DETAIL

chimneys

hipped roof   hipped Mansard roof   hipped M-shaped roof

Queen Anne bow window

Renaissance window   Queen Anne period window

Renaissance door

Queen Anne period door

JEWELLERY

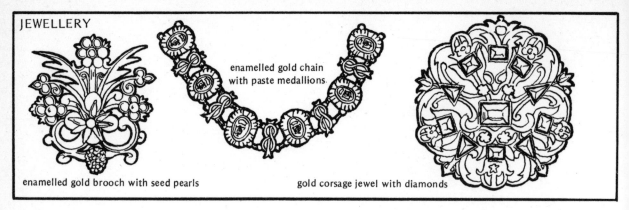

enamelled gold chain with paste medallions.

enamelled gold brooch with seed pearls

gold corsage jewel with diamonds

making lace

CUTLERY

carved ivory handles

KEYBOARD INSTRUMENTS

harpischord

spinet

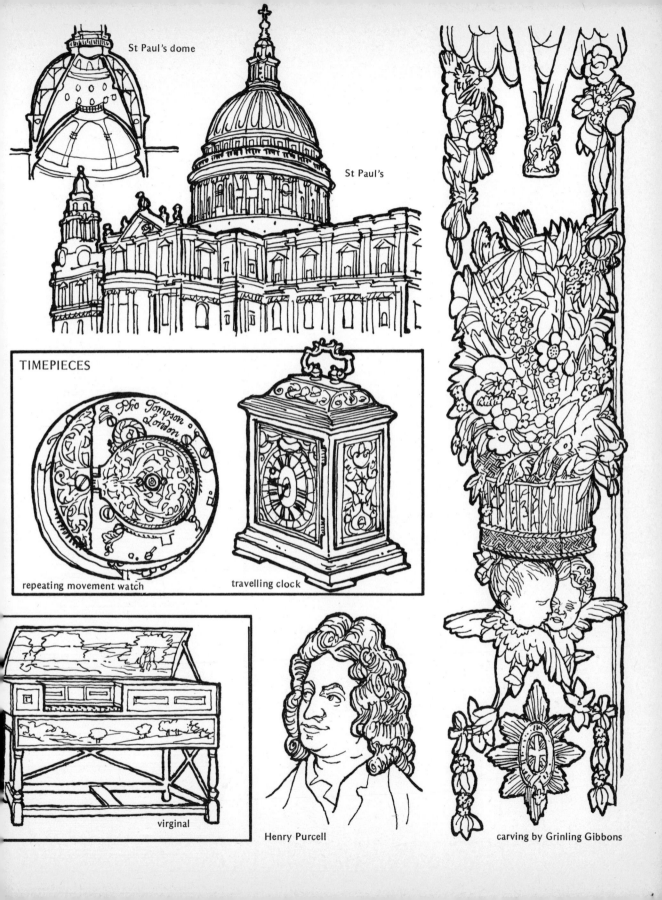

St Paul's dome

St Paul's

TIMEPIECES

repeating movement watch

travelling clock

virginal

Henry Purcell

carving by Grinling Gibbons

STUART TIMES **Some Important Dates**

1603	James I becomes first Stuart monarch
1605	Gunpowder Plot
1620	Voyage of *Mayflower*
1625	Charles I becomes king
1629	Charles begins 11-year rule without Parliament
1642-6	First Civil War
1649	Execution of Charles I
1653	Cromwell becomes Lord Protector
1660	Restoration of Charles II
	Foundation of Royal Society
1663	Milton's *Paradise Lost* finished
1665	Great Plague
1666	Great Fire of London
1688	Reign of James II ends in the 'Glorious Revolution'
1690	Battle of the Boyne
1692	Massacre of Glencoe
1694	Foundation of Bank of England
1702	Queen Anne becomes last Stuart monarch
1704	Marlborough's victory at Blenheim
1707	Union of England and Scotland
1714	Death of Queen Anne